To Rizzie —
On the occasion of a
beautiful afternoon at the
Art Institute, during a time
of much love and much growth.
With all my love,
Steve

GAUGUIN

Gauguin

BY RENÉ HUYGHE

"Bonjour Monsieur Gauguin"

CROWN PUBLISHERS, INC. • NEW YORK

Title Page: BONJOUR MONSIEUR GAUGUIN. Le Pouldu, 1889
Musée National Moderne, Prague

Translated by:
HELEN C. SLONIM

PRINTED IN ITALY   ALL RIGHTS RESERVED

INTRODUCTION

Study of a Nude (Seated Woman Sewing). 1880
Ny Carlsberg Glyptothek, Copenhagen

Although it was during the XIXth century that man first became conscious of his evolution throughout history, it was only during our century that was perceived the amplitude and brutality these changes could achieve. And art is the intensified reflexion of this.

At the end of the XIXth century, Impressionism closed one artistic era and opened up another one; it pushed realism to the apex of its achievement, but at the same time it signed realism's death warrant, for the vision of Nature which it offered to the public was too subtle, too "artistic," and the viewers did not recognize it as their own. Modern painting was born: from that time on it became less and less important to copy and to respect every appearance of Nature whose imitation had seemed, for centuries, art's supreme aim.

If the Impressionists contributed to this revolution, they did it unconsciously; they only started it rolling. It was the generation which followed them — around 1885 — which started, despite an admiration for them, to drift away and even to react against them, thus founding a new pictorial vision of which there had been no examples throughout the centuries. Among these new-comers, Gauguin had the most radical, perhaps the most fruitful courage. In June 1889 he was well entitled to write, from Tahiti, to Maurice Denis, who was taking place among the theorists of the new movement: « The first part of my program has yielded its fruit; today, one can dare anything, and furthermore, nobody is surprised. »

The generation of 1885 is responsible for the upheaval of traditional ideas: the artist ceased to believe he should obey Nature; on the contrary he considered that his creative part lay in the gap which separated the vision he offered from the normal one. But Gauguin alone knew how to serve this revolution with radical demands and a complete lucidity of aims and means. In this sense, he is entitled, more than anyone else, to be called the creator of modern painting.

*Portrait of the Maternal Grandmother of Gauguin
The Peruvian Flora Tristan*

GAUGUIN THE PRECURSOR

In a famous sentence, Gauguin stressed what separated him from the Impressionists: « They sought around with the eye and not in the mysterious depth of the mind. » This was the new problem which the team was to attack around 1885. They were conscious of their demands and of their assets; they offered to art a truth which no longer existed in the outer world, but only in the artist's mind and sensibility. However, not one of then dared go at it with as much resolution and lucidity as Gauguin.

Seurat, always tense, merged optical truth and abstract calculation of forms, where Nature fell into mathematical harmonies; Cézanne still respected and even sought the right sensations, but he could not separate them from his mind which released the notion of primordial simple and pure volumes, rigidly arranged. Through these two artists the mental contribution completed and heightened sensation to the point of beauty; but at no moment did the mind substitute itself for or contradict the sensation. Progressively, behind the veil of appearances which they dared not yet tear and throw aside, but which they only wanted transparent, they built up constructions of the mind; hidden by perception, the concept again took the profound importance of a skeleton, hidden by flesh which it holds together. They intimated, without yet authorizing it, the eviction of Reality by Plastic, which Cubism and the Abstractionists asked us to admire some time later.

Van Gogh for his part, like a tempest from the North, with no calculation whatsoever was butting with all his strength against a defected Nature and stirring it like a sea raised and ploughed by the wind, like a forest taut and buckling under a cyclone; he molded it in such a way that seeing it thus overturned Nature is forgotten and one is only conscious of the blast which distorted it. There, Reality yielded to Expression and a new trend was born which led to Fauvism and precisely to Expressionism.

Gauguin assumed both these trends toward Plastic and toward Expression which were emerging around 1885, and which were to rule the whole development of modern art. He took these trends with a definite audacity, only dampened by the atavistic concern to spare Reality, if not to leave it intact. He broke off from objectivity to which painting was compelled, thus deliberately breaking with six centuries of western tradition. He claimed the right to complete subjectivity, only keeping Nature's necessary material to imprint thought and sensibility.

He goes even further: by a *coup double* he found in this subjectivity the possible fusion point between plastic and expressive efforts which will divide modern art, and sometimes even pull it in opposing directions. It is because in both cases he gave the same answer: the assertion and personality of line and colour.

Perhaps less carried away than others by genius, he was all the more lucid, searching and determined. « With lots of pride, I finally got lots of energy and I have willed to will, » he said in a text intended for his favorite daughter Aline. His intelligent and stubborn strength took him still further, opened new ways for him, where Redon, alone in his time, had also entered. Further than plastic, further than expressing known feelings, he sensed the soul's submerged recesses, their untouched strength where an aging and refined civilization could bathe itself afresh. Odilon Redon used to say: « Everything is done by quietly submitting to what the unconscious brings. » Gauguin too will be fascinated by the unspoken, by the problem of its language; he will try and discover how to suggest the unspoken for lack of being able to explain it, how all that speaks to the feelings, line, colour, image, also speaks to the soul, and has a mysterious meaning which escapes reason, logic, and goes beyond them. Thus, like Redon,

*Pissarro: Portrait of Gauguin; Gauguin: Portrait of Pissarro, 1883
Drawing. Coll. Paul Emile Pissarro, Paris*

he anticipated the further developments of modern art, and half opened the door to Surrealism, (Hasn't the title of the Dada movement been suggested by a return to the « *Dada de notre enfance* — our childhood's rocking-horse » which Gauguin mentioned, rather haphazardly so as to be void of meaning?)

But beyond the school which undertook the systematic exploration of the unconscious, whose presence and importance he was one of the first to accentuate, Gauguin seems to have prepared still further extensions. Though fully conscious of all the emotive and plastic resources to which modern art dedicated and limited itself, though offering painting every possibility reducing art to this; he felt that painting can and must fully express the interior life, that it can be limited neither to sensations, nor to ideas, nor to emotions, but that it commits the soul and its mysterious complexity; nobody has used art to serve this soul, which from every part overflows the border of consciousness, more than did Gauguin. As well as any other, Gauguin satisfied the esthetic pleasure in which we wallowed during these past years, but he sowed both the necessity and the means of going beyond them. He never forgot the law of poetry which surpasses all others and demands that one's total humanity be pledged and satisfied, avoiding sterile pursuits. If this is the result of Gauguin's struggle and the heavy debt the XXth century owes him, he did not bring this wealth to light without unceasing and steady

GARDEN IN THE SNOW. 1883. Ny Carlsberg Glyptotek, Copenhagen

BRETON PEASANT GIRLS. 1886
Bayerische Staatsgalerie, Munich

MARTINIQUE WOMEN. 1887
Pastel. Private Collection

AROUND THE HUTS
1887. Martinique
Collection
Mr. and Mrs.
William Lee McKim
Palm Beach
Florida

The Grasshoppers and the Ants. About 1889
Lithography. National Gallery of Art, Washington D. C. Coll. Lessing Rosenwald

efforts, without a progressive conquest. Heavy, powerful and slow, now and then shaken by fever, primarily upheld by strength, Gauguin fulfilled himself only through patience. This bold and dogged energy was his pride and mainstay during his difficult and sometimes desperate life. It always galvanized him, led him, protected him from despair. He could write to his wife who was a prodigy of spiritual incomprehension as far as he was concerned: « I am working under unfavourable conditions and one needs to be a Colossus to do what I do under these conditions. » Up to his death he waged a hard campaign to obtain from life and from himself his personality and his art: « I willed to will, » he stated.

Pastoral Scene, Martinique. About 1889. Lithography

THE HARD AND SLOW VOCATION

He had to deserve everything, to assure himself of everything through will and strength, including his vocation as a painter. His rivals in fame knew how and wanted to be artists from the beginning, but Gauguin only discovered himself gradually. The sea was his first calling and he became apprentice and then sailor from 1865 to 1871. Then, looking for a job he worked for a broker as half-commission man; during eleven years he acquired some means through his financial job, and was even able to build up a collection of Impressionists. One day, the consuming monster of painting entered his life.

Through the habit of romanticising famous lives, this conversion has been envisaged as a brutal crisis, a sort of *coup de foudre*, an impulsive act, or as Somerset Maugham calls it « a spell » which tore him from his job, his home, his family obligations and threw him into a creative venture. It seems nothing of the sort happened. Gauguin, being of a slow, silent strong nature, had his dreams, of course, but he steadily strived to have them materialize. His whole life was nothing but a stubborn race toward a mirage, and recurrent disillusions, except in art. More space would be needed to analyse step by step the transmutation which changed a well-to-do and bourgeois stock-exchange broker into a pareo clad absolute artist who took refuge in mid-Pacific to lead the Maori's primitive existence. No breaking point, no leap, but a gradual and stubborn gliding.

In 1873 he married a Danish girl whom he met in Paris, Mette Gaad, a straightforward, practical, narrow-minded and hyper-conventional woman. They had five children in ten years. But painting crept in; he had learned to love it in his youth, through his guardian, Gustave Arosa, the collector. He met some artists, notably Pissarro, who was often a guest at his home, he started a collection, became an amateur Sunday painter, took part in the Salon of 1876 and was thus slowly driven toward the vocation which eventually consumed him.

In 1880 he rented a studio, on the rue Carcel, and joined the Impressionist group. He took part in their first exhibition. Three years in a row his canvases were shown and Huysmans, among others, was interested. In 1883 he reached the breaking point. Events followed swiftly: he quit the bank, although this decision does not seen to have been as free as has been alleged, as the financial crisis was causing many employees to be discharged. He decided to be only a painter. Life became difficult; Mette was not prepared to put up with sacrifices which seemed pointless to her, and when toward the end of 1884 Gauguin arrived in Denmark with wife and children, his in-laws were not too pleased. It has often been said that the artist abandoned his family to listen to the call of art. There again, as in the matter of quitting his job, the truth is slightly different: The correspondence between Mette and Gauguin, after they separated brings ample proof of the pressure that was made on Gauguin to force him to leave (I shall not go into details for lack of space). Would he, otherwise, have felt the right to write sentences like these, later on: « Now that your sister managed to make me leave... » « Your brother pretended I was in the way... » « I was struck a hard blow... » « I am put out of my own house... » « Don't worry about your mistakes being forgiven... » « Despite the way you hurt me, and which I won't forget...» and one day, April 3rd, 1887: « Today, I have no more resentment against you...»

What impresses one most in Gauguin's début is the absence of a spontaneous and self-assured creative power. He does not seem to be stirred by an inner devil demanding that he express himself and forcing the artist to discover his language at all costs. On the contrary, one perceives the patient application of a man who has a feeling that his work will achieve future greatness, but who still does not understand the nature of his art or the way to achieve it.

Gauguin wanted to be a great painter; he felt an undefined possibility in himself; his ambition was his art; he walked toward it as an explorer crosses arid lands to see the promised city disclose itself one day; but this art is not there, it does not pull at his heart and entrails only to demand expression.

Even when he returned from Arles, when he was definitely free from impressionism and when his final style could already be perceived in his works, Gauguin still hesitated. In a letter which its recipient, Émile Bernard, dates from Arles in 1889 and which was obviously written in Pouldu later in the year (1) Gauguin unveiled his doubts: « In my inner-self I think I can glimpse something higher. How I groped this year. My God (I said to myself) maybe I am wrong and they are right. This is why I am writing to Schuff (Schuffenecker) to ask your opinion so as to help guide me in the midst of my confusion. » Glimpse, grope, guide me, confusion... all these terms are quite expressive. But in another letter from Pouldu which Bernard dates 1890 and that various checking seems to place in autumn 1889, he added: « I am stagnating in a terrible sadness, and doing some work which will take a certain time to be completed, and I am glad not to go further in what I prepared before, but *to find something* more. I can

---

(1) One should be most cautious in admitting the order, origin and date of the letters published by E. Bernard; he is constantly misled by his memory and this source should be checked before used. For instance, he dates a whole series of letters « Arles 1889 » when Gauguin left this town at the end of 1888.

Head of a Breton Girl. Drawing. 1884. Former Collection Durrion

feel it, but *don't express it yet* (1). Under those circumstances my *groping* studies can only yield ignorant and clumsy results... What I want is a corner of myself as yet unknown. » Patiently and studiously he methodically explored the possibilities of a deep and receptive sensibility.

* * *

This is how he already was around 1875 and it may be interesting, having followed his career, to also follow the development of his art. When he started, he shaped a trade for himself. He had been inspired from the Impressionists whom he had collected, from Pissarro of whom he saw quite a lot and whom he chose as his master. His attitude was at first quite passive, although his stubborness seemed to predict a future blossoming: he accepted the program of the new school which, despite sharp contradictions in shapes, corresponded to the bourgeois' conviction of the end of the XIXth century: art is imitation, a reproduction of reality.

(1) Words in italic are underlined by the author.

SWINEHERD WITH YELLOW PIGS. 1888. Pont Aven
Collection Norton Simon, Los Angeles, Calif.

JACOB WRESTLING WITH THE ANGEL (Vision after the Sermon). 1888. Brittany
National Gallery of Scotland, Edinburgh

CHRIST ON MOUNT OLIVE (Self-Portrait). 1889. Brittany
Norton Gallery of Art, West Palm Beach, Florida

PORTRAIT OF MADELEINE BERNARD
1888. Pont Aven. Musée de Grenoble

THE ALYSCAMPS. 1888
Musée du Louvre, Paris

Study for the « Jeunes garçons. » 1888. Drawing

◁ «LA BELLE ANGÈLE.» 1889. Pont Aven
Musée du Louvre, Paris.

The quarrel, in fact, was only about the difference in opinion as to the means: traditional or new. Gauguin chose the latter, but not in the extreme; his colouring still remained the sober moderate shades which, from Bonvin and Fantin-Latour to Cazin and Bastien-Lepage seem to extend Millet's lesson of steady realism which Pissarro admired so much. Some canvasses of Guillaumin, Pissarro's friend and protégé, bear some analogy with Gauguin's palette. He knew him before leaving for Denmark and certainly felt some affinity with this man who, though painting, still kept his job as an employee.

Gauguin's painting, limited to grey or brown tones, lit by a few dull blues or some glaucous greens brings to mind a fat and compact humus, which will feed the seeds later deposited by will and an exacting intelligence, an humus and not a live substance like water or fire... Van Gogh, it is true, molded a still heavier clay in his first works; but his feverish hand shaped impatient convulsions which can be seen nowhere in this dormant matter.

This long phase of pensive sadness brought to both these artists inner revelations which could never be opened to the impressionists. And this sadness — no doubt, more than mere economy, which was only an added factor — will take Gauguin — as it did Nubien, Cottet, Dauchez, and Lucien-Simon — towards granitic, uncomplaining, solitary and gloomy Britanny where he first went in 1886. The Impressionists felt much more at home in the spruce, suburban *guinguettes* or the lively boat races at Argenteuil...

Gauguin, however, was only attracted by some of them: the masters who had made him love painting when he admired their canvases on the walls of his guardian, Gustave Arosa (1) — Millet, Courbet, Corot, Pissarro — predisposed him to prefer to the brilliant Impressionists, Monet and Renoir, with whom he never got along (*the Moulin de la Galette* is from 1876!), the more solid and solemn Impressionists: Pissarro (Huysmans at the 1880 Salon only saw in Gauguin « a dilution of the still uncertain works of Pissarro. »); Cézanne, who marked him deeply, up to the point of being able, later on, to reproach him with the theft of his « little sensation »; but although Gauguin knew him in 1881 in Pontoise to which Pissarro had made him come, what he had seen of Cézanne's by 1875 were sober-coloured, strongly built paintings like the « Hangman's House, » at the first Impressionist exhibition. And finally Degas, who protected him. None of these artists dissuaded him from this sad and solid style. What a contrast between « The Seine at the Iena Bridge, » with its dull and smothered winter painted by Gauguin in 1875 and the light-glittering river discovered by Monet, Renoir, Sisley and even Manet in Argenteuil. It was in 1875 that *Paris-Journal*, referring to the Impressionist sale of March 24 wrote about: « violet countries, red flowers, black rivers, yellow or green women and blue children. » This is far from the vision then offered by Gauguin... At the Independant Exhibitions of 1881 and 1882 Huysmans noted, seeing his « Sewing Woman, » his tense, Degas-like naturalism (« No one ever gave such a vehement note to reality. ») and in front of his « Studio » spoke of «his earthlike tonalities, his scurvy and dull colour. » And even in 1886, at the eighth and last Impressionist exhibition, Fénéon's sharp eye was struck by his « dull harmony. » He insisted on suggesting this heavy, almost sodden characteristic: « Dense trees shoot up from fat, rich and damp soil. »

(1) He was the one to get him the job with the stock-broker Bertin.

*Heads of Breton Girls. Dedicated to the Artist Maufra. About 1889. Pastel
Collection Mr. and Mrs. Emile Maufra, Levallois-Perret, France*

BIRTH OF A NEW ART

It was, however, around 1885 that the great venture, misery, nomadism, the slow conquest of genius, started. Already in 1885, when he was in Denmark, still trying to support his family by selling tarpaulin, when his painting was still struggling in the limbo of a dull impressionism, he perceived with lucidity an art which he was only to shape a few years later. As we shall see further, his January 14th, 1885 letter to Schuffenecker, confirms this. Let us therefore note: Gauguin is not the plaything of irresistible impulses coming from the depths of his inner sensibility; for him, creation is the consequence of thought.

As a matter of fact his painting career, that is, the cycle of his escapes, really started at this time: 1886: his first stay in Britanny, at the famous Gloanec boarding-house in Pont-Aven — his first artist's friendships with Emile Bernard and Van Gogh whom he met in Finistère and in Paris. 1887: the first escape across the seas with Laval, the first exotic experiment: Panama, Martinique; he returned to Paris in December. 1888: second stay in Pont-Aven. A new and decisive meeting with young Emile Bernard brought forward the doctrine of a new painting, at the same time Gauguin became a noted personality, almost a group leader. His first private exhibition took place at the Boussod-Valadon Gallery, where Theo, Van Gogh's brother was employed; the young painters started to consider him as the master of pictural symbolism and a rallying centre. In October of this same year, Gauguin went to Arles, answering Van Gogh's call, to try and build up an artists' community, a project which had long been in the Dutchman's mind; the idea was to alter both the material and moral conditions of art, « a renaissance, not a decadence studio » as he wrote to brother Theo before his friend's arrival. « By thus associating, each of us will be more himself, and union means strength. » Gauguin arrived around October 20th; on December 25th all hopes had vanished, all plans were anihilated. There had been the oft-told tragedy, Van Gogh's abortive murderous attempt, the cut-off ear, etc. Gauguin fled without again seeing his tempestuous friend who always felt bitter about this. At the end of 1888, Gauguin was back in Paris where he was more than ever considered the announcer of a new esthetic, especially after the exhibition held at the Café Volpini within the Universal Exhibition's program. In April 1889, he was back in Pont-Aven; but in October he prefered settling down at Mlle Henry's Inn at Pouldu, which was less crowded. One after the other he worked at the « Yellow Christ, » the « Breton Calvary, » the « Belle-Angèle, » and, at last, he acquired full possession of his art: vision, plastic, technique were defined with the same authority. After staying in Paris from December 1890 to the spring of 1891, where he was welcomed at the Café Voltaire, Gauguin finally left for Tahiti on April 4th, thus opening the final twelve-year span during which his destiny and his art were to be fulfilled.

* * *

During these five years, however, Gauguin had already come out of his first phase of mere, almost passive observation; the consciousness of plastic means had slowly emerged. His shapes still kept something compact, some clay-like power, which he originally had borrowed from Pissarro and Millet. After that, Cézanne, this other silent man, had contributed by his example to Gauguin's touch; he now wanted it tight, monotonous, with parallel, almost stubborn, hachet-like strokes; this arbitrary craft helped him to put off reality, to become conscious of pictorial independence. In turn, his line breaks free: it extends, unwinds, becomes unbroken, independent, shading. He is helped by the firmness of trees, the design of branches, of trunks, and also, again, by Cézanne's example. But he was more influenced by Puvis-de-Chavannes and the Japanese prints. The latter, especially, provided him with the model for an art which called for decorative form and which, though respecting the level of the image, refused to break it with false depths, with false relief, and preferred to expand the line and spread colour areas. Gauguin, also, refused to sacrifice to imitation and make-believe; on the other hand he had to heighten their suggestive power. Therefore he did not only develop the arabesque possibilities of the line, but also equivalences of expression. So Gauguin can be considered as a precursor of Toulouse-Lautrec who will also ask from Puvis and the Japanese the secret of this double aspect of the line.

It is always interesting to observe the surroundings a painter requires: on the walls of the Studio in Pouldu, Seguin told us, Gauguin had hung reproductions. Every one of them reflected an anxiety to bring out the design's harmony and continuity. There was Manet's « Olympia » (the famous joke about his « playing card » painting and the importance he gave to shading should be remembered); the most graphically lissom Italians: « The Annunciation » of Angelico, Botticelli's « Spring » and also decorative motives by Puvis and some prints by Outamaro... He met Puvis and talked with him; in 1889 he still put him on the list of the great artists which he wanted invited to his exhibition; and the same year he copied his « Hope » in the background of a still life. He also often mentioned Japan, and like most Impressionists, put some Japanese prints in some of his canvases, as in the Schuffenecker's family portrait, for instance.

Head of a Peasant Girl. The Fogg Museum of Art, Cambridge, Mass. U.S.A.

« *L'Arlésienne.* » *1888. Drawing. Collection T. E. Hanley, Bradford, Penn. U.S.A.*

If not Puvis, Japanese prints prompted him to the use of colour, of splashes, of flats. When he first tried exotism, when escaping from misery, seeking the unknown, he had gone to Martinique in 1887, among bitter disillusions, he had at least discovered the density of tones under more luminous skies. From this time on, his colours were more and more definite, intense, violent — never light or flickering. His inner solemnity continues to set him aside from the Impressionists' vivacity.

When he came back to Britanny for the second time, in 1888, his new esthetic asserted itself, showed off and was provocative. Nature was definitely tamed and did not raise her voice; meekly she submitted to the imperative transmutation which had forced her out of her three-dimensions into the two-dimensions of the canvas where the line and coloured area would now live by their own laws. Gauguin knew it: « I am not a true-to-life painter, » he wrote in 1900 to Emmanuel Bibesco, « today less than ever, » and that same year in a famous article in *l'Occident*, the new generation's spokesman, Maurice Denis, recognized that during the days of Pont-Aven « he freed us from the chains with which the idea of copying (nature) had bound our painters. » On this day, modern esthetic, with all its boldness and possibilities, was born.

But is Gauguin truly the author of this revolution?

Emile Bernard unceasingly protested, and claimed the honor. Up to the last, Gauguin felt quite bitter about it. Who was the initiator, Gauguin or Bernard? Who invented the synthesis which Gauguin, who hated theories spelled: *Synthese*: « *Saintaise* because it rhymes with *foutaises* (nonsense) »? (1). Historians gravely and at length discussed the problem and arrived at various conclusions. One thing is certain, even before meeting Bernard -« the little Bernard » who was only twenty- four years old and whom he welcomed as would a master already surrounded by disciples — Gauguin was steadily marching towards the affirmation of the power of line and colour, freed from Nature's constraint; it is also certain that the new doctrine did not bring anything which had not already been realised in the Japanese prints which Gauguin loved; moreover, it is certain that at the beginning of 1885, in his letter to Schuffenecker dated January 14, Gauguin stated the theory of the symbolically expressive powers of line and colour, which supposes that he was conscious of their free use. But, on the other hand, it is true that Gauguin's closed and dreamy psychology always progressed gradually, leaning on whatever support it found in external events; he had neither the dogmatic mind nor the definite confidence which Bernard will later develop and which will drive him to repudiation and to extreme and resolute positions.

Anyhow, of what importance was an influence for this great man? No more than the revelation of a form in which he could etch what he already carried in his heart and for which he was seeking expression! Gauguin knew perfectly well that Bernard had not brought him anything which he did not already have and with which he was not already preoccupied. Bernard, on the other hand, could prove that such and such a day, at such and such an hour, he had offered Gauguin a « system » for painting, in which his aspirations had suddenly become attainable. The quarrel is pointless. Bernard did not change Gauguin's destiny as a painter, but he gave him the syntax he needed for his language; the only thing that matters is what Gauguin finally handed down to us.

(1) Gauguin, so sensitive to thought, was highly suspicious of theories and the false molds into which they forced creation to shrink. Although a " symbolist " himself, deep inside he made fun of the movement and its dogmatism. Monfreid told with a smile, that he approved of Verlaine, saying ironically at the Café Voltaire: « Oh bother! they annoy me these " cymbalists! " »

Study for the Painting on Page 37. Beginning 1891. Drawing

THE SYMBOLIST DOCTRINE

In any event Gauguin knew where he was going, at least since 1885, from his letters to Schuffenecker on January 14th and to Denmark on May 24th. In these letters, although he was getting into a phase of pictural doubt, he nevertheless already expressed symbolism's program.
 He fully appreciated the surprising novelty of this program; it upset him: « I sometimes feel as though I were crazy. » he wrote in the first of these letters. And this is what he disco-

SEWING. 1889. Pont Aven
Collection Emil G. Bührle, Zürich

31

SELF-PORTRAIT OF GAUGUIN, BEFORE THE YELLOW CHRIST. 1890. Brittany
Formerly Collection Maurice Denis, France

▷

THE CALVARY (After a painting by Braspard). 1889. Le Pouldu
Musées Royaux des Beaux-Arts de Belgique, Brussels

STILL LIFE WITH ORANGES. 1890. Brittany
Collection Brown-Bovery, Baden, Switzerland

STILL LIFE WITH HEAD-SHAPED VASE AND JAPANESE WOODCUT. 1889
Le Pouldu. Ittleson Collection, New York

BRETON LANDSCAPE. 1889
Collection Emil G. Bührle, Zürich

FLOWERING OF SPRING. 1891. Paris
Collection Walter P. Chrysler, Jr., New York

The Family Schuffenecker. 1889. Paris. Former Matsukata Collection, Musée du Louvre, Paris

vered: lines and colours have not only the power to reproduce what we want, the reality which Nature's appearance shows us, but they also have an emotional power which can convey a mood to the viewer. « There are noble lines, false lines... a straight line suggests infinity, a curved line limits creation... Colours explain still more... Some tones are noble, some vulgar, some harmonies suggest tranquility, some console you, some excite you into doing something bold. » The same thing for shapes. In an orchestrated art, « it is the most intimate part of man which comes to life, veiled. » This is capital, Symbolism was hereby founded, before Emile Bernard, before Aurier !

So Gauguin is the inventor? Let us not go so fast ! In all this can be found strange connections with what Baudelaire — and before him the man who inspired his artistic thought, Delacroix — thought and asserted. In one of his projects for the preface of *Fleurs du Mal*, Baudelaire explained in the same way that the poetic phrase is capable of suggestion, just as « a horizontal line, a straight ascending line or a straight descending line, » that it can « go right up towards the sky without becoming breathless or perpendicularly down to hell as fast as any weighty object, » etc... Developing this dual possibility of language and plastic, he explained that in poetry and in art there was a « possibility of expressing any feeling of sweetness, bitterness, beatitude or horror. » In his *Curiosités Esthétiques* he had perceived that Delacroix's works showed this mysterious power: « the wonderful chords of his colour often lead one to dream of harmony and melody. » And Gauguin wrote further, in that letter quoted above: « A deep feeling can immediately be translated: dream over it, seek its simplest shape. » Clinging to this affective quality of shapes, he also specified that it was in the order of... feeling. « Everything is there in this word, » « feeling expressed before thought » and which, without thought, and with its own means conveys « the most delicate and visible emanations of the brains... all the human sensibility. » Moreover, wherever Delacroix's mind left its mark, one could find the birth of the same ideas: in Odilon Redon, in Gustave Moreau, who said similarly: « the evocation of thought through arabesques and plastic means, this is my aim. »

As for Gauguin he went on pondering, and on May 24th he stated the consequences of his reflection for art; first of all, realism, which so far had seemed art's main function, should be opposed: « Nothing but painting, no deception. » Therefore the design does not need so much to reproduce reality as to express the message which the painting carries. The stroke... is a way of emphasizing the idea. » It is worth noting that Gauguin's trend of mind reached that of Maurice Denis, who in *Theories* expressed it thus: « To stop reproducing life and nature through approximations and improvised deceptions, but on the contrary to reproduce our emotions and our dreams by expressing them through harmonious shapes and colours; I persist in believing this was a new position. »

So, as soon as the beginning of 1885 Gauguin transferred the motive of art as reproducing visible appearances of nature, to « the idea. » It took another three years before Albert Aurier stated in the *Mercure de France* that from now on « a work of art will be ' idealist,' as its sole ideal will be to express the Idea. »

Despite this quarrel for priority, which was sometimes waged with a certain harshness, art's new concept was to assert itself in minds and in works during these few years before 1890.

In 1886, Paris had welcomed Van Gogh who had forcefully emerged from the cocoon of his first manner and Britanny had welcomed Gauguin who had settled in Pont-Aven, had freed himself from the influences of his beginning, and had created « Synthetism. » Five years later, the new school which had formed around Gauguin was disclosed to the public at the Café Volpini during the Universal Exhibition of 1889. It definitely repudiated Impressionism, took the opposite course, and reached out to the parallel movement of literary Symbolism. 1884-1889, five years ! From the Independants to the Café Volpini — a complete overturn had taken place.

The same revolution, the same need to break with the past, to escape from tradition, was taking place at the same time in literature: in 1885, René Ghil started the battle by publishing his *Traité du Verbe*; the next year he founded the Symbolic and Humanist School, as Moréas was giving the *Figaro* his manifest on *Symbolism*. Favorable influences were converging simultaneously: in 1884 E. M. de Vogüe revealed the Russian novel, in 1885 the *Revue Wagnérienne*

Portrait of Stéphane Mallarmé. 1891. Etching

was first published. The anti-naturists' proliferation took place around the same period: 1884, the subversive *Revue Indépendante* and *Tâches d'Encre* by Barrès; 1886, the *Pléiade* and the *Vogue* where Laforgue appeared, *Symbolisme* by Gustave Kahn and Moréas, *Décadent, Décadence*; in 1889, the year of the Café Volpini, the *Plume* and *Mercure de France* first appeared. This is also the period when Verlaine settled in Paris and revealed his *Art Poétique*, when Mallarmé opened his salon, when Huysmans edited *A Rebours* and Laforgue his *Complaintes*...

From then on, for fifteen years, with fierce energy and stubborness, sinking into solitude, far from civilization, Gauguin was going to change the traditional basis of art, disclose possibilities which are nowadays still being developed. Amidst pain, misery and adversity, he was to break the shackles which bound him and his contemporaries, and was to teach freedom to the art of the future. Before 1900 he had forebodings of what was being accomplished: « I think that despite the great number of clever characters and of humbugs the beginning of the century will bring quite a beautiful crop of art. » And proudly he already reckoned what this art would owe him: « Martyrdom is often necessary for a revolution. My work, considered as to immediate result, » he stated modestly, « is of little importance compared to the final and moral result: painting is now freed of all its chains, of this dreadful amalgamation forged by schools, academies, and especially mediocrities. » (1).

(1) To Dr. Gouzer, March 15th, 1898.

Tahitian Woman. 1892. Drawing

Head of a Girl - Tahiti. M. Knoedler Gallery, New York

TAHITI
AND THE QUEST FOR ORIGINS

In the spring of 1891 Gauguin left Paris, renewing his unsuccessful Martinique venture, this first try to escape a rotten civilized world. This time he had decided to go further in quest of the mirage of origins and of purity, as far as the Pacific islands. He noted (1): « On June 8th, after sixty-three days of crossing, sixty-three days of feverish waiting, we saw strange fires zig-zagging on the sea. »; it was flagrant Tahiti, *Noa-Noa*; Tahiti, delightful land, *Nave Nave Fenua*. But the small provincial-like capital, Papeete, showed him nothing but a derisive imitation of the civilization he had rejected and which had already preceded him over there, « an absurd, almost caricatural imitation of our customs, fashions, vices and civilized absurdities... To have travelled so far to find this, this which I was running away from ! »

So one morning, Gauguin left in a car borrowed from an officer, drove for forty five kilometers and settled down in Mataïea district. « On one side the sea, on the other the mountain... Between the mountain and the sea is a bourao wood cabin... Berween the sky and me, nothing but the large, tall fragile roof, made out of pandanus leaves where lizards hide. »

Soon, however, Gauguin's loneliness bore in upon him; he made friends with his neighbours, but:
« In the shadows of the pandanus leaves
You know it is good to love. »

And one day he went on a search throughout the island; in the mountains, throughout the valleys; then on a horse borrowed from a gendarme, he trotted to the eastern coast. In Fanoé, he was invited to alight and to eat: « You seek a wife? Do you want my daughter? » asked the Maori woman; fifteen minutes later she came back with a « tall, slender, vigorous child. » It was Tehura. « This child, about thirteen years old (corresponding to 18 to 20 in Europe) charmed, awed, almost frightenend me. »

They both went back to Mataïea. « Then started a fully happy life. » Slowly Tehura led him to « a full comprehension of her race, » by life's daily teaching... « Through her I am beginning to grasp a number of mysteries which have been so far incomprehensible to me. »

Gauguin was about to try an extraordinary experiment, to put off the old European man, to break off with the esthetic, the inspiration and the style of a gradually sclerosed civilization, « this deceptive and conventional European civilization, » and to go back to the sources, where he hoped to find man's truth again. This is usually considered as the supreme effort of escape brought about by an exasperated individualism, a desire to break off with acquired and passively respected traditions, the striving of a personality eager for freedom towards liberation and independence.

This might not be quite accurate. By more and more strongly asserting the rights of his conscience and lucidity, that is, of his independence, of his won aptitude to conceive and direct

---

(1) This quotation and the ones that follow are from *Noa-Noa*.

Spirit of the Dead Watching. Monotype

Woodcut of « Pape Moe. »

PAPE MOE (Holy Water.) 1891-93. Tahiti
Collection Emil G. Bührle, Zurich

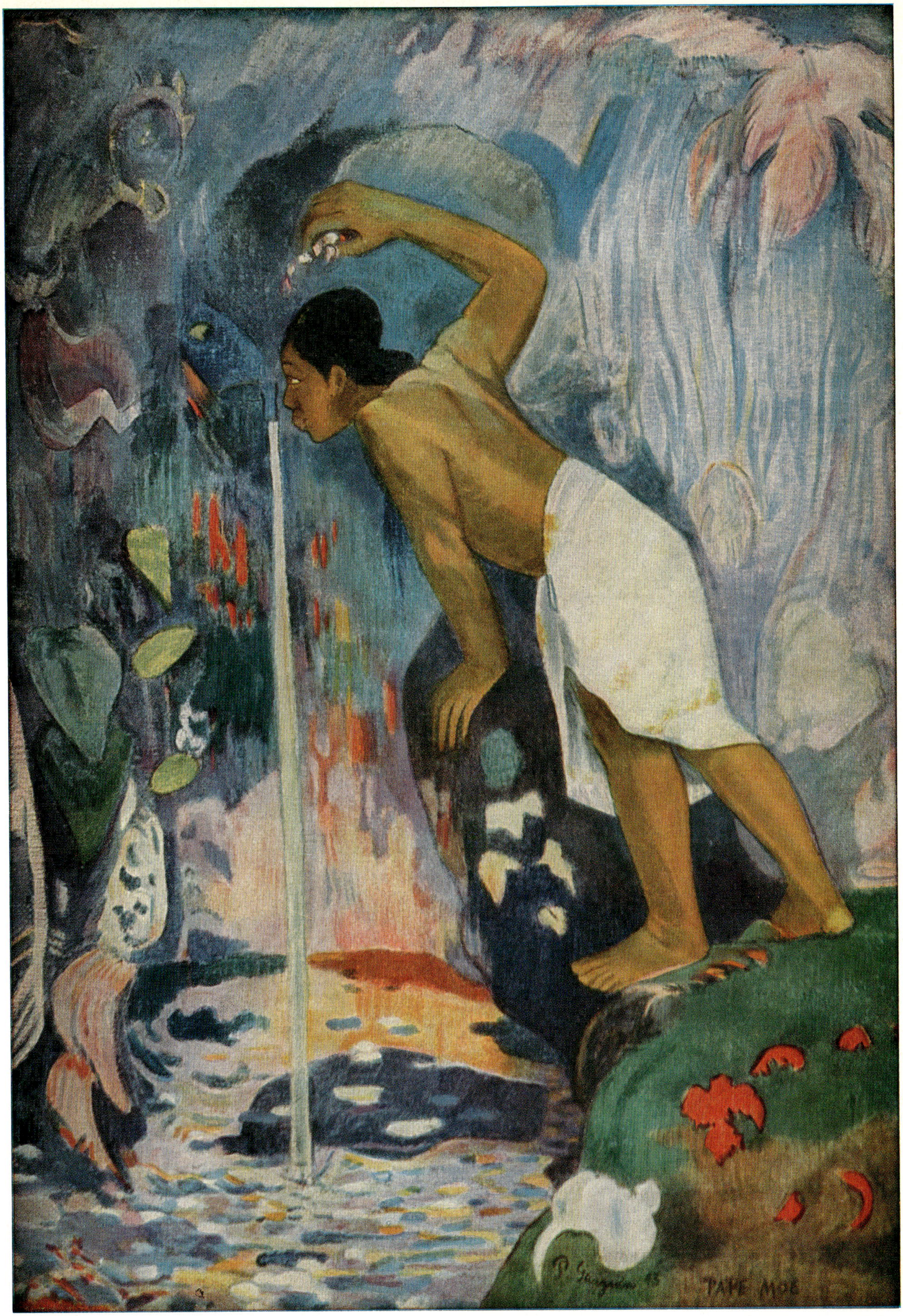
PAHE MOE

TAHITIAN LANDSCAPE. 1891
The Minneapolis Institute of Art, Minneapolis, Minn.

TAHITIAN WOMEN ON THE BEACH. 1891
Dresden Museum

TAHITIAN WOMEN BATHING. 1892-93. Collection Robert E. Lehmann, New York

I RARO TE ORIRI (Under the Pandanus). 1891. Tahiti
The Minneapolis Institute of Art, Minneapolis, Minn.

VAHINE NO TE VI
(Girl
with Mango)
1892. Tahiti
Formerly Degas
Collection
Baltimore
Museum of Art
(Cone Collection)

TE AA NO AREOIS (The Seed of the Areois). 1892. Tahiti
Collection William S. Paley, New York

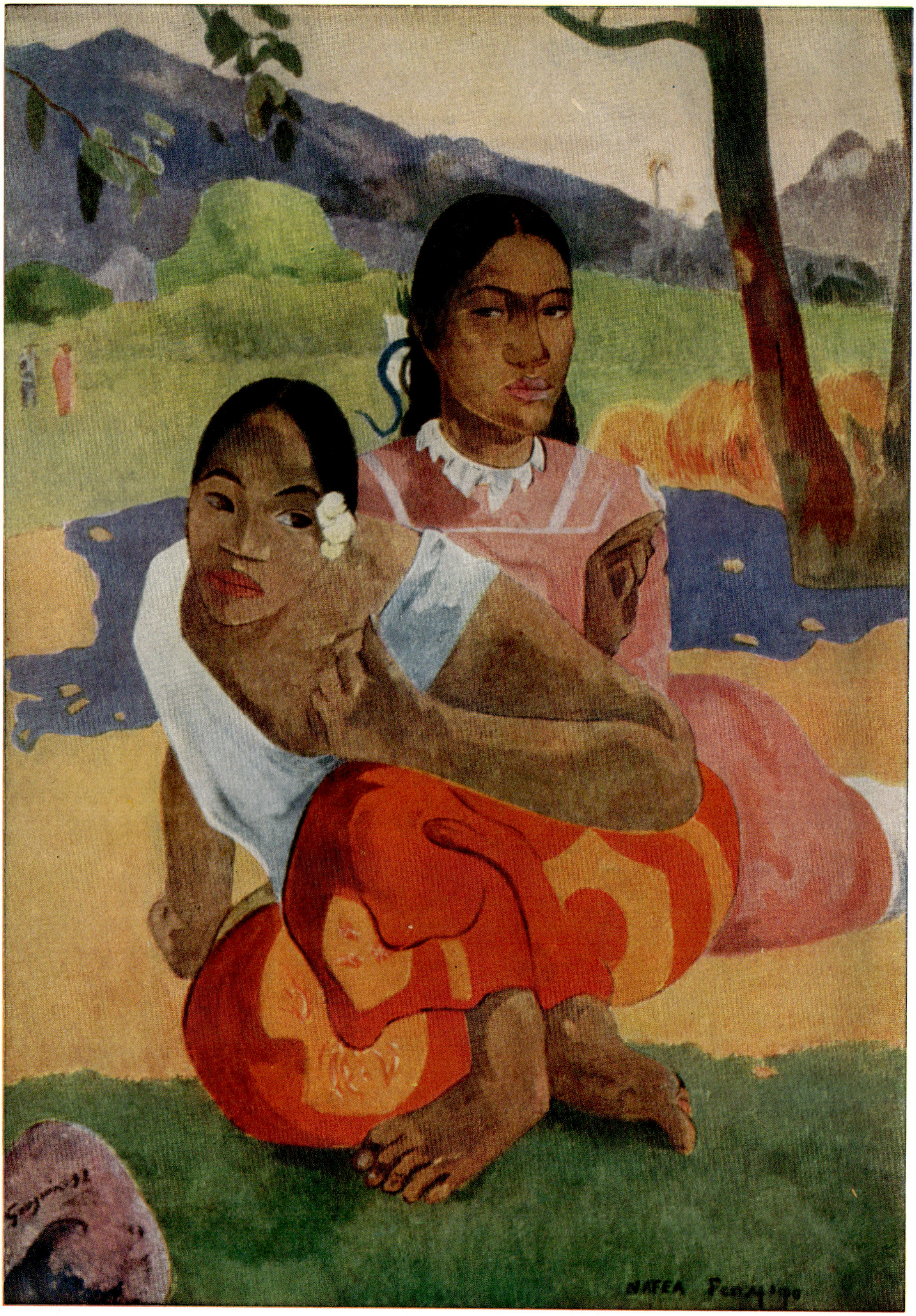

Tahitian Girl. About 1892. Study for the Painting on opposite page

◁

NAFEA FOA IPOIPO (When Will You Marry?) 1892. Tahiti
Collection Rudolph Staechelin (on loan to the Basle Art Museum.)

55

Manao Tupapau. The Spirit of the Dead. Woodcut

himself by his own logic, modern man has gradually severed the heavy chains which bound him to his collectivity. He is uprooted, not from earth but from humanity. And the modern ailment, the crisis of saturated individualism, the instinctive return to collective passivity, might only be obscure gropings in order to pull oneself together and to branch again on to the trunk which gives out the only sap. And, if one studies it closely, that is what Gauguin instinctively sought. Modern, civilized society seemed no longer capable of fulfilling its role in regenerating and feeding individuals; only conflict could be raised; and Gauguin declared that he rejected the « Parthénon horses » and wanted to come back to the « *dada* of my childhood, » the « good old wooden horse. » He aspired to find an undamaged humanity, a humanity whose full breasts could pour out the vital element from which man seemed to have been prematurely weaned.

The whole of the first part of our century endeavoured to ruin rationalism and replace it by « a quiet submission to what the unconscious brings, » as Redon worded it, to shake liberalism and replace it by dirigism, to reset up collective imperatives — though they be blind — against personal freedom, and to resolutely shape the social structure along these lines. Doesn't that show the reaction and fatality of a world which had been dragged by excessive experiences into individualism, and which tried, sometimes to excess, to sweep back in the opposite direction? Gauguin, so often a precursor, was secretly perturbed by all this. Therefore he perceived a certain moral health in what civilized man contemptuously calls the *barbarian* and the *savage*, a primordial purity, a saner and more normal state of human condition. This haunted him. So he escaped successively to Britanny, to Martinique, to Tahiti, to the Marquesas Islands, always further.

So Gauguin was to be the first — before Picasso and Derain, *discoverers* of African art — to get his inspiration from primitive peoples. In 1887, at Martinique he was still faithful to the more or less impressionist naturalism of his beginnings; he was obviously under no local artistic influence. In Britanny, in 1888 — helped by Emile Bernard's doctrinal assertions — he took the plunge and dropped the scruples of the realists; the influence of Japanese prints strongly helped him in this respect; from now on his canvases are mostly a play of lines and colours, *assembled in a certain order*, to use Maurice Denis' famous expression. But will he not be diverted towards decorative painting? It was in 1889, at the end of his stay in Britanny, that the old Breton calvaries gave a soul to this style still in the limbo, and whose shape threatened to fall into the *modern style*. A fierce, primitive soul, a presence of what is sacred and its mystery, came back to life again in the midst of decadent realism. Let us compare two canvases painted this same year: *The Little Nude Breton* amd the *Calvary*; the plastic order which was already emerging from the naturalism is transfigured, struck by a religious solemnity, a perception of an unknown god beside which he will soon be looking for the traces of primitive soul which he wanted to renew in himself. This attraction to something sacred breaks out in the background of his portraits which he wanted to put in expressive harmony with the faces, according to the symbolic thought which also inspired Van Gogh. In 1890 he set up the *Yellow Christ* behind his own effigy; around Meyer de Haan, he set strange anguished faces whirling, and entitled the canvas: *Nirvana*. Christianity and Buddhism, to which he has often referred in his writings, are not the only ones calling him. He is not attracted by dogmas, but by the impact of what is sacred, the meaning of which is lost in our time, even in religion. For him, what is sacred is linked with a notion of obscure, virgin and barbaric power. The Idol will bring him what God no longer gave him.

Title of the Revue « Le Sourire. » 1889. Woodcut

*Nave Nave Fenua
(Delicious Earth.)
Tahiti. Woodcut.*

*Noa-Noa
Woodcut*

Manao Tupapau. The Spirit of the Dead Watching. Paris, 1894. Lithography

THE BARBARIC SOURCES

Even the year before, in 1888, he placed the first of his idols, motionless and mysterious near the *Belle Angèle*. What is it? He no doubt was inspired by the anthropomorphous ceramic, with its detached often stirrup-like handles, which can be found in Northern Peru, in the Chimu art's area. Some vases from the Chancay valley are somewhat close to these shapes. And one must not forget, that according to Gauguin himself, there was « some savage » in him: his grandmother was the famous Flora Tristan, born in Peru, daughter of Don Mariano Tristan y Moscoso, Spanish colonel serving in Lima, and niece of a viceroy. His great-aunt was married in Bogota, Columbia, and thus linked him with the Uribe family. » There are two natures in me, » Gauguin wrote to his wife, in 1888, « the Indian and the sensitive. » It was the primitivism's spark which he tried to light again, out of the ashes of his unconscious.

When he was three years old in 1851, he had been taken to Peru by his father who died during the trip, and had spent four years in that country with his mother and sister. One can imagine the deep and terrifying impression some of these Mochica vases — which were everywhere, even in his home — made on him and how his childhood questions and dreams — seeds of adult

Head of a Girl - Tahiti

Tahiti. Study. Monotype

MAN WITH AN AXE. 1891. Tahiti. Collection Mr. and Mrs. Alex L. Lewyt, New York

SIESTA. 1893. Tahiti
Collection Mr. and Mrs. Ira Haupt, New York

THE MARKET. 1892. Tahiti
Kunstmuseum, Basle (Donated by Dr. Robert von Hirsch)

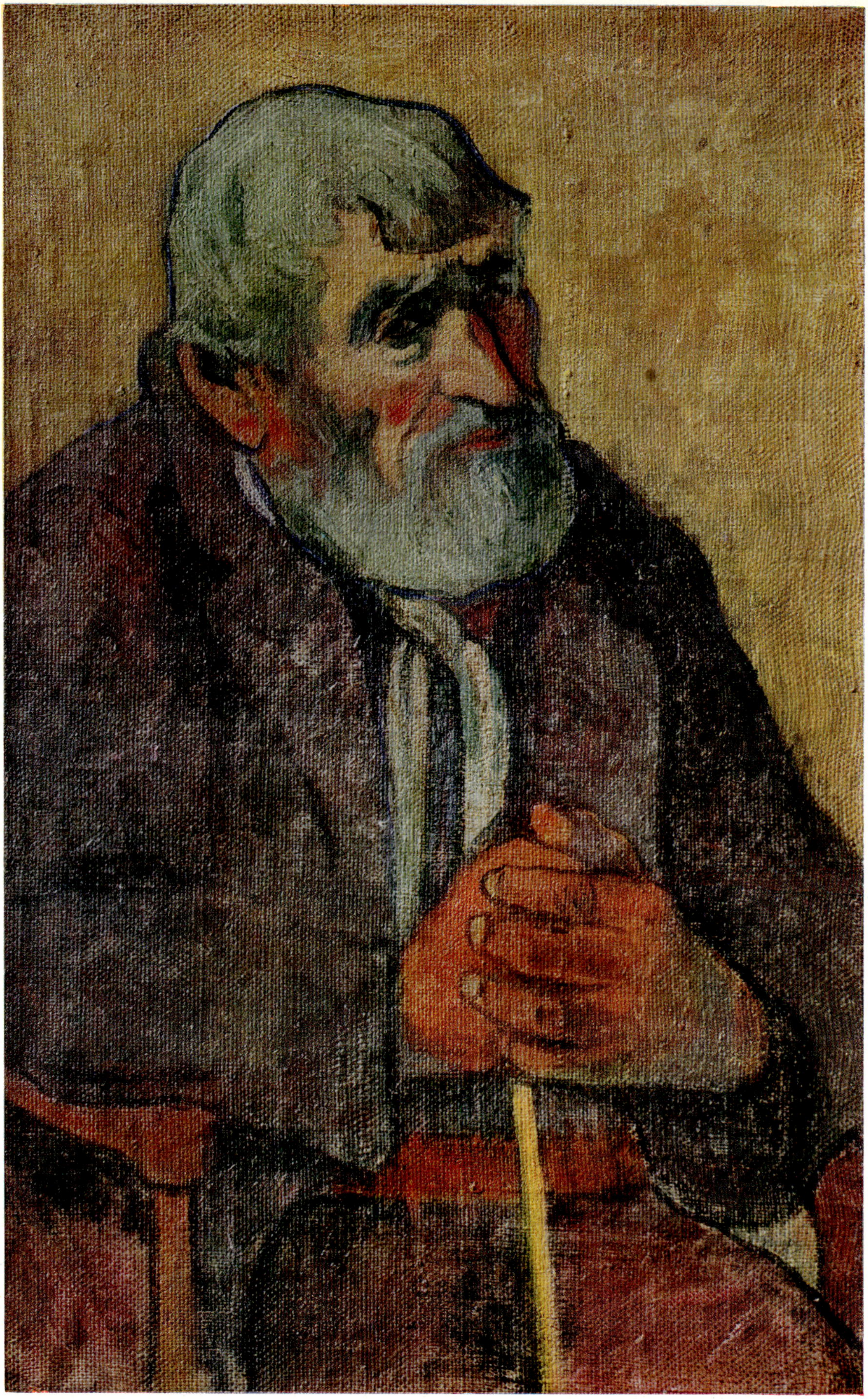

Te Arii Vahine. Woman of Royal Family. About 1896. Woodcut.

ones — took hold of these images. An obscure attraction, the magic of childhood's memories brought him back to these strange and, for him, doubly fascinating images. « Old time gods have kept a home in women's memories » he wrote one day, but also in children's...

Furthermore there is definite evidence from Gauguin himself that he knew these Peruvian vases. In *Before and After* he notes: « My mother had kept some Peruvian vases and also a number of figures made out of solid silver, just as it comes out of the mine. It all disappeared in the Saint-Cloud fire which the Prussians had set. » So he grew up and lived until he was twenty-three years old in contact with these strange objects. He found some also at the house of *Père Maury*, » this French industrialist who had made a fortune in to Lima by selling the cemeteries these enormous monstrosities which the too prolific Italian sculptors could not get rid of. « I saw again in Paris this very old père Maury... He had a very nice collection of vases (Incas' ceramic) and lots of jewels in solid gold made by the Indians. » (1)

In 1889 an event occured which matched Gauguin's still nebulous curiosity. Near him, already the « spirit watches, » the spirit of barbarian gods. The Peruvian vases, with their somewhat good-natured realism, are not enough to give it shape. But the Universal Exhibition — which was to show the public Gauguin's and his friends' new synthetist tendencies at the Café Volpini's exposition — also showed the painter a set of pre-Columbian works, mostly Mexican, especially castings: he studied them carefully and made a number of drawings. He also studied the art of certain decorative scripts, especially Mayan art which provided him with many examples, among which straight lines meeting perpendicularly made designs somewhat like disorganized fragments of a Greek key-pattern. This vision, entirely different from the European one, prepared him for the somewhat closely related one Tahiti was to offer him. In the same way, some simplified treatment of the human face, such as can be found in Zapotecous art, taught

(1) *Before and After.*

◁
MAN WITH A CANE. 1893. Brittany. Petit Palais, Paris

Tahitian Woman Sitting About 1896. Pencil. The Art Institute of Chicago

him some schematizations, like the one where eyes and mouth are indicated by a kind of almond cut by an horizontal line.

So when he landed in Tahiti, in 1891, his memory already carried a stock of *barbaric* shapes. How much of it would he find again here? Here, where there was no metal to make tools of, no clay to make ceramics! Wood carving and cloth painting were the only possibilities offered to artistic creation. Furthermore the Tahitian parthenon is not very anthropomorphous. Tahora and the gods descended from him remained symbols of the universe, of earth, of heaven... So Polynesia with its already quite evolved religion, did not really deem it necessary to represent them. In the West, in Samoa, in Tonga, geometrical decorations were the only ones to be found. In Eastern Polynesia, from the Hawaïs to the Society Islands, passing by the Marquesas Islands, where Gauguin eventually died, there are some effigies of gods; however, not daring to represent the supreme God, art is limited to the *Tiki*, a conventionalized image of the male and fertilizing principle which could be found on the handles of working implements, as well as in stone statues: even if, according to tradition, these statues had been as high as 4 meters (like the Easter Island ones) there were only some small ones left in Gauguin's time. Moerenhout who left a very complete study of the Pacific Islands, around 1803, tells us that the Atouas, set amongst the superior gods, had their stone or wooden images placed at the top of the Maraes, sort of temples which Gauguin mentions. To these images called *Toas* were added the *Tiis*, inferior gods, which Gauguin also describes; these more carefully carved figures were set

Adam and Eve. 1900. Monotype

on the temple's limits as if to guard it, and were in the same fashion erected on the shore, facing the sea. The huge mysterious statues of Easter Island whose significance is still discussed, seemed of the same kind and seemed clearly explained by this ancient Tahitian custom. Gauguin mentions them in his *Ancient Maori Cult*, he noted their huge sizes, and there is no doubt that he took advantage of this information, inspired by the small statues which he saw, to imagine them enlarged and monumental in his paintings, although he actually had found none. So he never really saw this enormous, monstrous and stupid Idol with head drawn back into shoulders and hands folded on stomach, which he painted in many a Tahitian scene; but he considered he had the right to build it up again from the small or middle-sized effigies which one can now see in *Le Musée de l'Homme* in Paris.

Gauguin's exotism implied much less imaginative fantasy than is usually supposed. The odd stylization of eyes, hands, etc... which he sometimes painted are in accordance with the Tikis', which had been constantly used to decorate the most common objects and which were finally reduced to geometrical lines. We know that Gauguin studied them closely: the manuscript of *Noa-Noa* (1) contains pasted pieces of tracing paper; they are prints made by rubbing a pencil on the paper set against the raised engraved surface of decorated objects. Tikis' elements can be recognized: heads, or silhouettes with arms on the stomach; also the simplified shape which Gauguin, as we saw, gave to the hands of his divinities.

On the other hand, the cloth he painted escapes all decorative order; there again, Gauguin is accurate. Polynesian cloth (the *tapa*) made by the continued pounding of barks' inner fibers with a grooved mallet, showed a much less abstract ornamentation: it was made by pressing on the cloth, so that they would be printed, plants, briars and even objects, which had been dipped in a red or yellow dye extracted from tree bark.

To conceive his barbarian gods, Gauguin did not only seek inspiration in his pre-Columbian memories — which introduced him to Pacific's art — but he carefully studied Polynesian art, in its representations as well as in its abstract stylizations.

When Gauguin returned to France in August 1893, penniless and sick, he settled down in a studio, in Paris, 4, rue Vercingétorix, with Annah the Javanese, a mulatress whom he had found wandering in the street and who soothed his nostalgia for faraway lands and races. According to his friend Paco Durrio, Gauguin had decorated his new home with numerous Polynesian works, which he had brought back, especially idols « carved in unknown red, orange or black woods. » (2)

---

(1) Noa-Noa - page 168 and 169.
(2) *Cossio del Pomar* « La vida de Pablo Gauguin. » Catalog of Gauguin's retrospective exhibition, Paris-Latin-American Association, December 1926, Paris.

Menu Illustrated by Gauguin (The Commissaire Dindon and a Policeman.) Watercolour

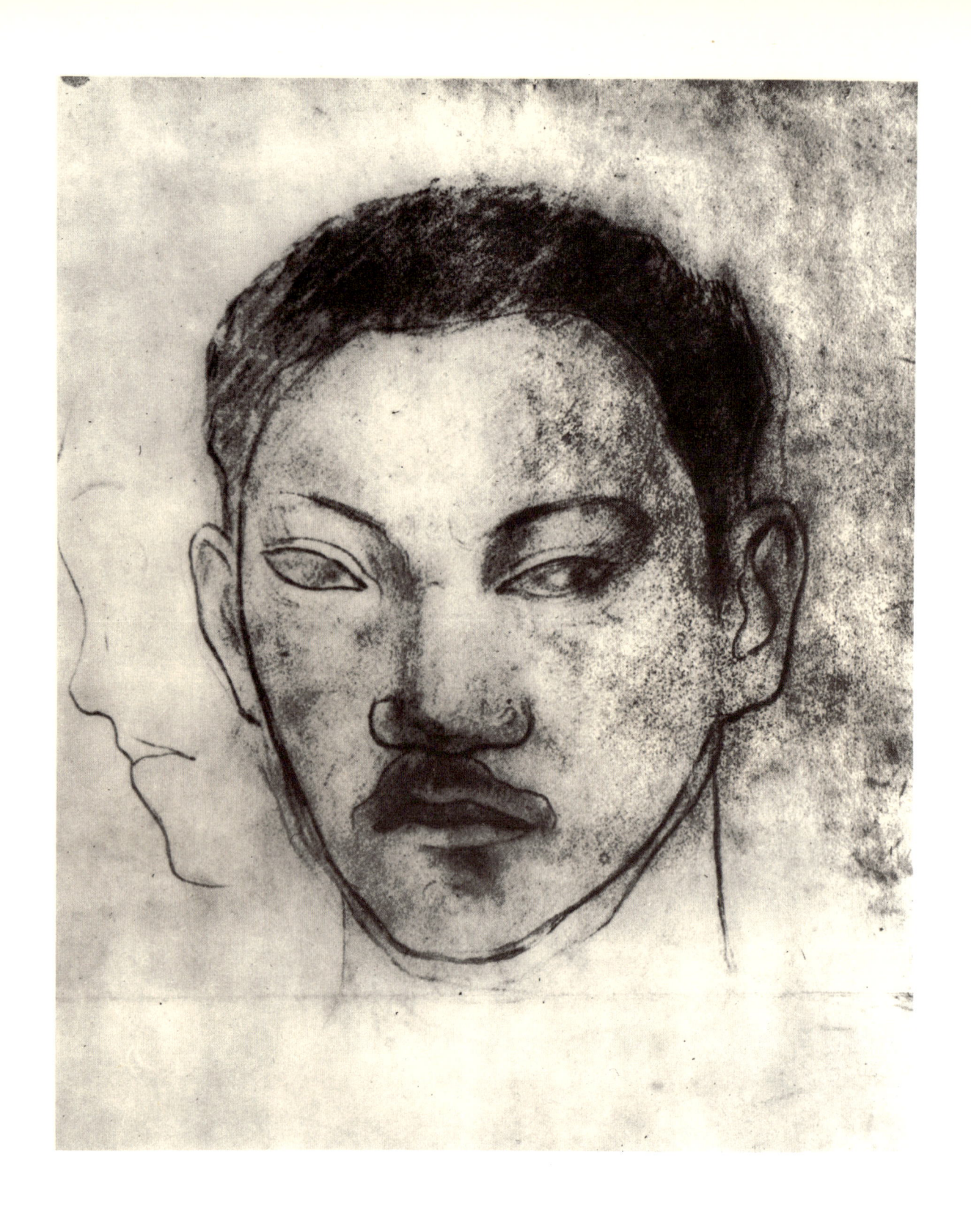

Studies. Head of a Tahitian and a Profile Sketch. Drawing

THE LAST STAY IN THE ISLANDS

After a last meeting with his wife in Copenhagen, in 1894; after having gone back to Britanny, the following April; to Pont-Aven, to the Pouldu and to Concarneau, where he got his ankle broken in a stupid fight about Annah whom he had taken along, Gauguin came back to Paris in December and decided to return to Tahiti. After his disastrous sale at the Hôtel Drouot, on February 18th, 1895, he sailed towards the Fragrant Island.

Deceptive reality was awaiting him again in the place where he was pursuing his dreams. It took only two years before, in January 1898, he tried to commit suicide. In his despair he had been toying with the idea for several months.

Exhausted by moral and physical misery, deserted by his wife, who only thought of selling the paintings he sent her without ever allowing him any part of the proceeds; wounded to the depths of his heart by the death of his beloved daughter Aline, about which he learned in April '97; ruined, hard pressed, unable to reimburse this year's loans from the Agricultural Office, fearing to be sold out; sick, tortured by his leg which never got well since the accident in Concarneau, by eczema which ate him up, his sight impaired by a double conjunctivis, his life threatened by a badly treated syphillis, worn out by blood spitting (now far from the mirage of Tahiti « delightful land » !) Gauguin had been speaking of killing himself since June. In December his mind was made up. With unbelievable courage he wanted to put the final touch to his work: he made his pictural will: *Whence do we come? What are we? Whither are we going?* He worked at it « during the whole month... day and night with an outrageous fever »; and he completed the book where he had noted the essentials of his written message: « In January 1890. » He took to the mountains « where my body would have been eaten by ants » and stuffed himself up with arsenic; but he took too much and was sick to his stomach; this saved him, and « after a night of dreadful suffering, » he went home.

Life went on, and so did his work. In August 1901, Gauguin settled down in the Marquesas Islands, in Antuana; he built « the house of Pleasure » which he decorated with his carved woods, added to his painted work. But the lack of money and physical suffering were made worse by a permanent, incessantly aggravated conflict with authority, from the gendarmes to the bishop. By speeches and through the paper he edited and illustrated, *Le Sourire* (The Smile) he induced the natives to revolt against the discipline they were subjected to and which slowly destroyed in them the soul of their ancient civilization. In the midst of these worries which gradually weakened him, he painted his last masterpieces: *And the gold of their bodies..., Barbarian Tales*, which followed the ones painted in Tahiti and among which *Ia Orané Maria, The Spirit of the Dead Watches* (painted during his first stay), *Nevermore, The White Horse, Woman and Mango* (painted during his second stay) are considered the most famous. Sentenced to jail and to a fine, on March 23rd, 1993 for having « accused a gendarme » (« these worries are killing me, » he wrote to Monfreid), he is found dead on May 8th. His posthumous life had started.

GAUGUIN AND THE OCCIDENTAL WORLD CRISIS

Beyond Gauguin we have the problem of our civilization's evolution and of his place therein; the problem of civilization, which Gauguin brutally expressed in 1895 to a great Occidental intellectual, Strindberg. He felt « a whole impact between your civilization and my barbarity. You suffer from civilization. I am rejuvenated by barbarity. » In the twilight of an aging civilization, didn't Gauguin « the Savage from Peru, » Gauguin « the Indian, » as he called himself, draw the ways through which it can and will try to escape from itself, to burst the limits which smothers it?

He perceived and definitely delimited the conflict: he revolted against ancient culture, against this Greco-Latin tradition which founded Europe but which was dying of its own sclerosis. He was not alone: more clearly and more categorically than another, due to the accident of his origins and genius, he expressed a worry which came to light with the romantics and which, as we saw, made fast progress thereafter. « Decline of the West » said Spengler, condemnation of Latin culture, claimed Gauguin. He will repeat this ten times, for example to D. de Monfreid in October 1897: « Always bear in mind the Persians, the Cambodgians and a little bit the Egyptian. (1) The great error is the Greek, however beautiful it might be. » What shocked him in Puvis, although he admired him? « He is Greek and I am a savage, a collarless wolf from the woods. » (2) No more Pegasus, no more Parthenon horses! One has to go back « far back, further than the Parthenon horses — as far as the *dada* from my childhood, the good old wooden horse. » (*Before and After*). This is not a sally, it is a message. And anyhow « these blasted Greeks who understood everything » they themselves taught that « animality which we carry in us should not be as despised as is said, » for « they imagined Anteus who got back his strength by touching the earth. Believe me, the earth is our animality. » and it is our unconscious! Anteus Mythe! Wasn't it high time to renew it? This is the question Gauguin asked from his whole work.

Thus didn't he already express the dominating problem of our times? Didn't we for the past year witness our civilization's dramatic effort go beyond the limits of over-organized thought, to find again beyond an over-codified culture, the primordial soil, this unconscious which nowadays obsesses literature, art, philosophy, psychology, even medicine — all of modern life? isn't the passionate curiosity which carries us towards unfashioned psychisms, close to their origins, towards primitive arts, negro or archaic, towards children's drawings, Sunday painters, madmen's works, a sign of the instinct and nostalgia which drives the modern world, seeking regeneration, towards origin of thought? To get there it realizes it must burst and transgress rational discipline, a corset which built its strength but which choked it when it started to grow.

Gauguin, like a prophet, tried to find out, through art, where the pain was located. « Primitive art, » he stated, « comes from the mind and uses nature. The so-called refined art comes from sensuality and serves nature. Nature is the servant of the former, the mistress of the latter... she degrades the mind by letting herself be adored. This is how we fell into naturalism's abominable error. » In his opinion this race towards naturalism chaining the Mind started with the Greco-Latin civilization: « Naturalism starts with Pericles' Greeks... In our present misery there is but one way out: it is to come back frankly and reasoningly to the principle, » that means to « primitive art. »

Gauguin's thought might be misunderstood. It is obvious that Greece in Pericles days safeguarded the Mind and ignores materialist realism to which its later followers were to succumb. However, Gauguin's view is almost accurate: it is with Aristoteles' thought, his care about the

---

(1) The painting « Te Matete » (Basel) is of significance in this respect. The silhouettes look as if they were from the Nile.
(2) This sally was Degas', Gauguin secretly flattered, often repeated it.

MATERNITY
1896. Tahiti
Collection
Mr. and Mrs.
Edwin C. Vogel
New York

TAHITIAN WOMEN BATHING. 1897
Barber Institute of Fine Arts, Birmingham, England

VAIRUMATI. 1897. Tahiti
Former Matsukata Collection, Musée du Louvre, Paris

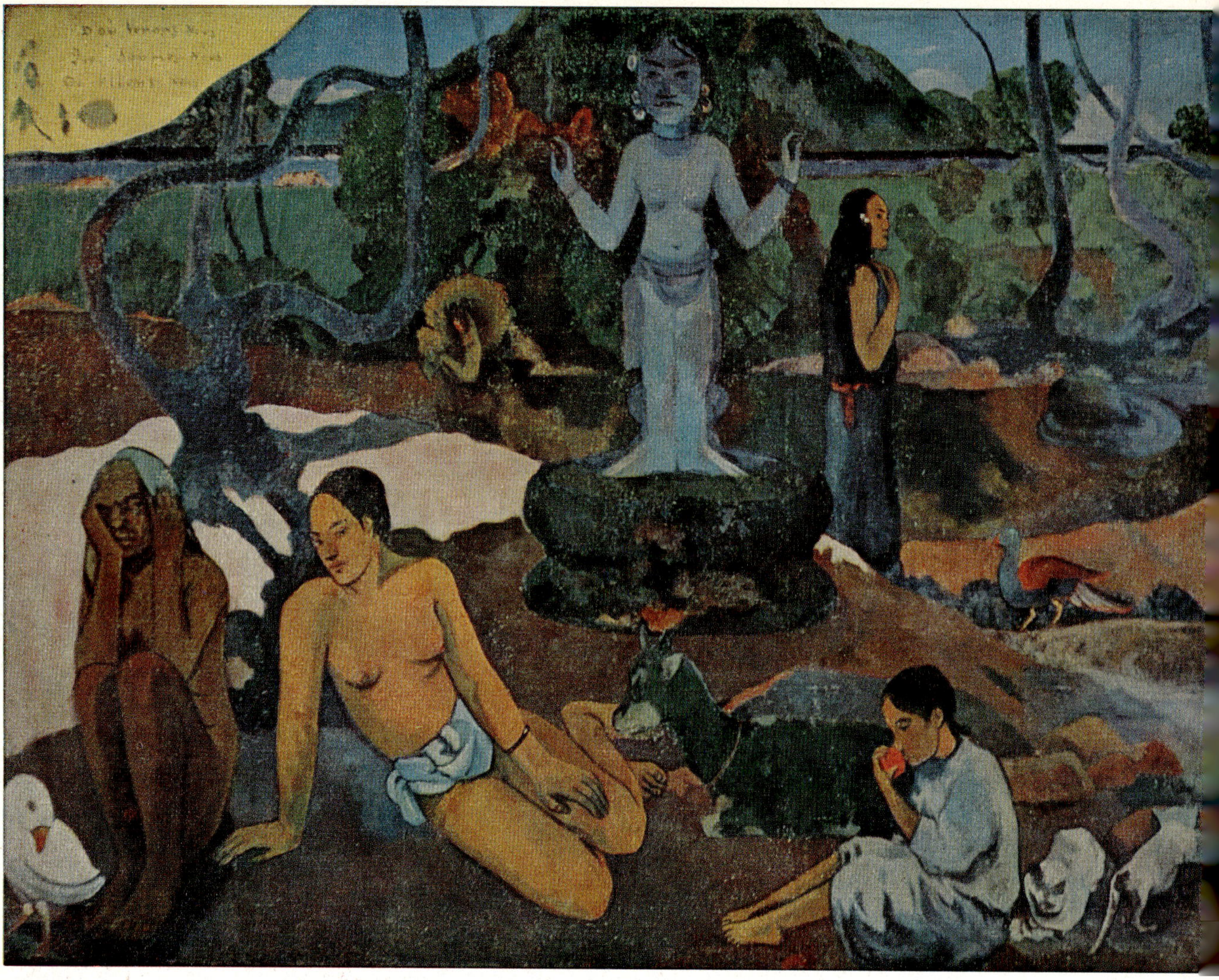

WHENCE DO WE COME? WHAT ARE WE? WHITHER ARE WE GOING? 1897. Tahiti
Museum of Fine Arts, Boston, Mass.

STILL LIFE WITH SUNFLOWERS. 1901. Tahiti
Collection Emil G. Bührle, Zürich

TAHITIAN LANDSCAPE WITH GIRLS. 1901
Collection Emil G. Bührle, Zürich

POÈMES BARBARES. 1896. Tahiti
Fogg Art Museum, Harvard University, Maurice Wertheim Collection

BARBARIC TALES (Vision of Meyer de Haan in the background). 1902. Tahiti
Folkwang Museum, Essen

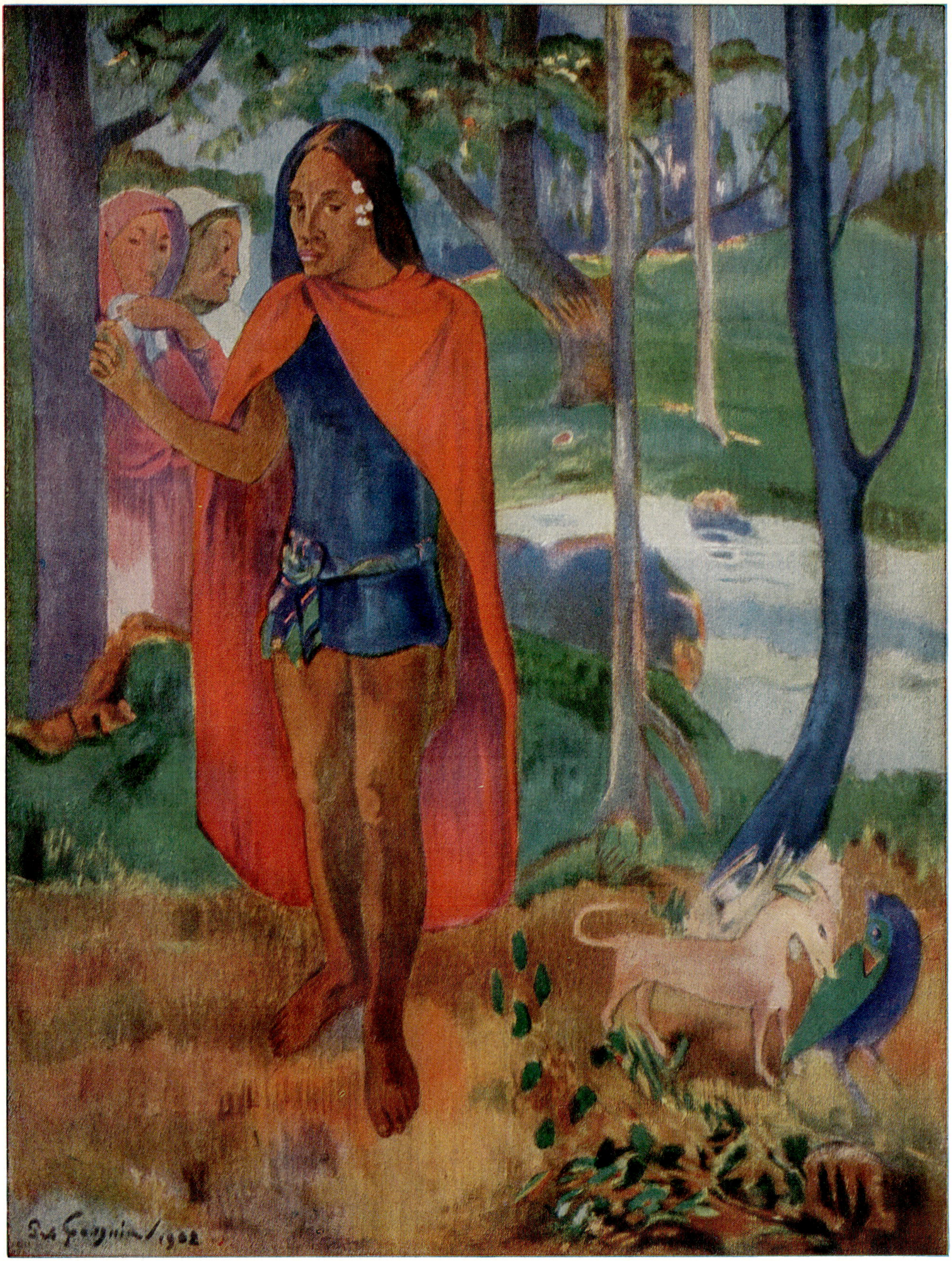
P. Gauguin / 1902

Head of a Tahitian Woman

◁ ON THE MARQUESAS ISLANDS. 1902. Private Collection

particular and experimental fact affixed to the idea, Plato's beloved, that a new concept was rooted: it gave us our certainties, our successes, but also our lacks, our limitations which so many primitive or oriental civilizations ignore.

Since that day, Occident endeavoured to give knowledge a stable and universal basis, an objective basis: it was found in the outside world, common origin of our sensations, and in order to be safer, it primarily considered this outside world under its material and spatial aspect which was easier for observation and measurement, outside of time which is constantly modifying its identity. It tried to establish constant connections of cause to effect between these thus defined phenomena, to explain them, to forecast their repetitions and allow their imitation or improvement. Culture thus based on objective elements, on concrete facts and logical connections strived to limit itself therein, thus choking and rejecting the rest, all these inner, subjective revelations which jeopardized the universality of positive reality on one side and of reason on the other.

Rome then dulled and systematized this culture: Deeply shaken during the High-Middle Age by the fall of the Empire, and the onrush of barbarian elements, it gradually got back its hegemony since the XIIIth century with the revival of Aristoteles and the rising of the bourgeoisie. From then on, the two columns of the temple were: sensation and logic, reality and reason.

Starting with the XVth century, bourgeois positivism, especially in the North, Latin renaissance, especially in the South, gave it an increasing rigidity, and it found its expression, its instrument, its triumph in Experimental Science. Gradually the sense of Beauty and Harmony which maintained Greece's balance and spirituality, faded out; gradually the overflowing of the soul with which Christendom had regenerated our era, got disfigured. Harmony or Faith, everything yielded to the dogmatic rule. The XIXth century brought about the triumph of the bourgeois pressure with naturalism and of the Renaissance pressure with academism. The binomial Reality and Reason became the only and absolute formula.

From the beginning of the XIXth century many a mind concerned itself with the withering and suffocation felt everywhere; the drying out of the inner life's spring and of its renewal was witnessed with awe — especially after the rational sensualism of the XVIIIth century; one was horrified by the sterilization which degraded the Greco-Latin tradition and made it day after day narrower, more restricted, mostly under the action of the middle-class law.

Then a desperate effort was made to break this continuously narrowing circle where the soul threatened to be asphyxiated, and it was Romanticism. A great effort was made to reach the soul. Up to that time the main arts were those where matter and space with all their weight and stability, played the leading part: architecture and sculpture. Classical painting, such as Davidism, aspired to catch up with these and transpose them. As a reaction, music, which moves outside of space and only in time, a suggestive and no longer a descriptive art, art of the inexpressible and invisible, was turned to. (As Gauguin wrote to Monfreid: « All told, painting should seek suggestion more than description, as does music. »)

Gradually Time became important again and so did the irrational, not only in the literary and artistic field, but even in Science (1) which found an extraordinary surge through this escape since the end of the XIXth century. Nowhere is anything conceived anymore without its changing, fleeing, dynamic notion, like the principle of music. Colour, which was much closer to it than the spatial and rigid line, has become painting's main concern.

But in order to attain this liberation, points of support had to be found; to escape from the narrowed latinity, it was necessary to look beyond its frontiers. The time had not yet come to resort to Oceania, as Gauguin did. At first Orientalism was enough; nearer even, the Northern or Germanic powers were called upon; better than others they had kept safe from the rational and realist ascendency — this was the hour of Shakespeare, Byron and the German Romantics — In the past, one went back to the periods which had best freed themselves, and the Middle-Age was rediscovered. As for Gauguin, he brought this escape to its extreme limits with one stroke; in space he sought up to the antipodes, in time beyond all memory.

---

(1) This Science which the philosopher Roy nowadays considers as « scandalous for the Reason's principles of a former time. »

The Spirit of the Dead. 1900. Monotype

Oviri. Profile of Gauguin. Bronze Relief. Private Collection

«Be in love and you will be happy» wrote Gauguin in 1889. Woodcut ▷

88

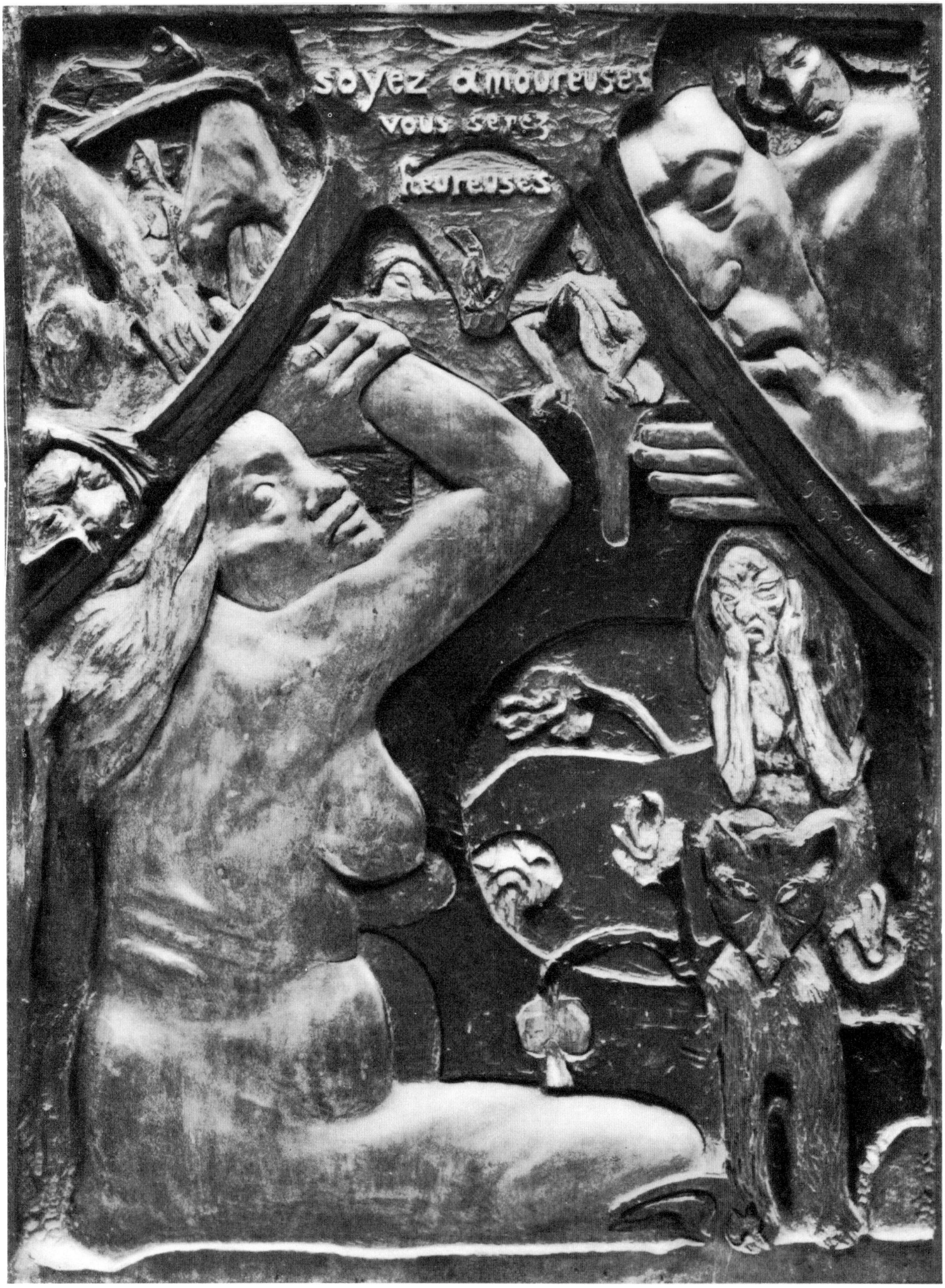
soyez amoureuses
vous serez
heureuses

Profile of the Artist. Drawing

THE DISCOVERY OF MODERN SOUL

But another principle had to replace the one that was being rejected. To the new XIXth century Germany whispered the new epoch's pass-word, this *Stimmung*, which Novalis who liked it so much considered as « indicating, predicting psychical conditions of a musical nature. » The *Stimmung* was indeed the denial of rationalism, the first groping effort towards its adversary, the unconscious; the *Stimmung*, that is, all that escapes definition as well as explanation, all that escapes from fixity, all that is felt instead of understood, all that belongs to soul's dark and infinite part rather than to logic's clear and limited field. From now on, one was going to endeavour to apply less the definable rules of Beauty than to express irreplaceable (1) surge of sensibility's outpourings. Romanticism liberated all this and Gauguin had foreseen it, inherited it, over and above the realist's reaction. He broke free from rationalism and settled into the soul's unlimited, confused and exhilarating universe. « And night has come. All is quiet. I close my eyes *to see without understanding* the dream of infinite space flying before me... » (2)

Dream and imagination as opposed to reality, time and its invisible dimension preferred to dull, motionless areas, the inexpressible to definition, the unknown and the strange to certainties and principles, what else was there to break away from? Wasn't logic's firmest basis the intangible principle of causality: to explain and understand each thing through its cause and effect? In outlining the game of analogies, Romanticism, Germany, then Delacroix and Baudelaire, had

(1) « Love that will never be seen twice, » said Vigny. What else did impressionism do?
(2) Letter to Fontainas, March 1899.

started erecting a whole system of knowledge of the world, of perception and explanation which it did not grasp, similar to the one used by primitive peoples with their magic means. Gauguin aspired to these relationships which intuition discerns and logic ignores, to these mystical links connecting one feeling to another, an appearance to an idea, nature to man and which weave a web of inexpressible communion; he recognized them in symbolism; but to make sure they wouldn't escape him and degenerate into some false literary doctrine, he sailed toward primitive lands where they still ruled unpolluted by reason and its deductions.

Indeed, Delacroix, was the first in France to perceive it, and he planted the seeds: he opened for us Pandora's box, and elusive intoxicating perfumes spread out and diluted into the air, all the new powers: intensity, imagination, colour, music, correpondences, suggestions, mystery... But Delacroix was still shackled: he was a man of high classical culture and thought more of reviving than of ruining traditions. He did not go any further.

The first to be conscious of a rupture from which the modern world would emerge, the first to have escaped Latin, European civilization (with Rimbaud, however!), to find again primordial impulses among barbarian tales and savage gods, the first to have lucidly and radically dared to break off with and repudiate outer reality and rationalism, was Gauguin. Some took a more direct part in shaping modern art, as we know it in our century; nobody, however, has more strongly helped the human soul to dare be itself, as we see it today following its ever unpredictable development. When Occidental art used the known as its pole, Gauguin gave it the unknown as an aim, towards which, young Rimbaud, alone, had launched his *Bateau Ivre*.

It is rather vain to ask who was the greater, Cézanne or Gauguin, Gauguin or Van Gogh. Perhaps, however, the creative urge surging from the depths of the being and which imposes itself on the world, was not as demanding in Gauguin as was his avidity to discover. In a way he did not so much follow his path, pushed forward by his own inner surge, as incessantly drawn forward by the ever-unsatisfied mirage of the unknown. Throughout his life and his development, he was in pursuit of an eternal else.

But it is essentially in this that he foreshadowed and represented our time which does not so much know what it wants as what it desires to escape from.

By so deeply expressing the modern soul, its impatient repudiations, its anxious avidity, in a word, its anguish, Gauguin struck a chord which will always sound in man's heart. By breaking free from sometimes too controversial certainties, one is prepared to face emptiness; but then one discovers the problem of destiny and its awesome grandeur.

And Gauguin is among the poets and artists who have been able to lead us to the brink of our own enigma. Perhaps the point of this enigma has never bothered us as strongly as during the centuries where

Profile of the Artist. Drawing

man has deliberately thrown down obsolete armour which no longer fits him. The XIXth and XXth centuries are these.

During the XIXth century Delacroix took pleasure in bending Hamlet's pallor and affliction over Yorrick's answerless skull.

As the XXth century approached, Gauguin went far to find « in dreaming eyes, the cloudy surface of a fathomless enigma. » He put this enigma before us when he vainly sought death in attempted suicide, on a canvas where three blaring cries seek an answer:

« *Whence do we come? What are we? Whither are we going?* »

BRETON VILLAGE COVERED BY SNOW, 1903. GAUGUIN'S LAST WORK. MUSÉE DU LOUVRE, PARIS

BIBLIOGRAPHY

PUBLICATIONS BY PAUL GAUGUIN

c. 1890   *Notes Synthétiques*, published by H. Mahaut, *Vers et Proses*, July-September, 1910.

1892   *Ancien Culte Mahorie*, manuscript in the Louvre's collection, reproduced with a study, « *La clef de Noa-Noa*, » by René Huyghe, La Palme, Paris, 1951.

1893   *Cahier pour Aline*, Tahiti, Library of Art and Archaeology, Paris.

1895   *Préface à l'Exposition d'oeuvres nouvelles d'Armand Seguin*, February-March, Paris.

From 1895 on   *Noa-Noa*, manuscript in the Louvre's collection, published in collaboration with Charles Morice, Revue Blanche, October 15, 1897, then by De la Plume, 1900, again in 1908, finally by Crès, Paris. The manuscript has been reproduced in facsimile by Meier-Graefe, Berlin, 1926, and by Jean Förlag, Stockholm, 1947. On the manuscript in the Louvre collection Gauguin wrote, following *Noa-Noa*, *Diverses Choses*, 1896-97; *Notes éparses sans suite comme les Rêves, comme la Vie toute faite de morceaux; souvenir d'un hiver de '86 et d'un hiver de '94, l'Eglise catholique et les Temps modernes*; and at the end, « fin du volume, Janvier, 1898. » Reproduction of a sketch given to Morice, Sagot-le-Garrec, Paris, 1954.

1897-1898   *L'esprit moderne et le catholicisme*, another manuscript, City Art Museum, St. Louis, discussed in summer 1949 bulletin of the museum.

1899-1900   Gauguin published some articles in *Les Guêpes*, Papeete, and in *l'Indépendant de Tahiti*. He himself edited *le Sourire*. Nine issues and three supplements reproduced in facsimile, with introduction and notes by L. J. Bourge, Perret Maisonneuve, Paris 1952.

1902   *Racontars de Rapin*, manuscript, Falaize, Paris, 1951.

1902   *Avant et Après*, published in facsimile, Kurt Wolff, Leipzig, 1818, and by Druet, Paris. Crès, Paris, 1923.

LETTERS BY GAUGUIN

1918   *To the Danish painter Willumsen, les Marges*, March 25.

1919   *To Daniel de Monfreid*, with a tribute by Victor Segalen, Crès, Paris, 1919, and Plon, 1930 and 1950 (edition established by A. Joly-Segalen).

1921   *To André Fontainas*, Librairie de France, Paris

1926   *To Emile Bernard*, Tonnerre; Nouvelle Revue, Brussels, 1942, Geneva, 1954.

1939   Roger-Marx - *Lettres inédites de Gauguin et de Van Gogh* in *Europe*, February 15.

1943   *To Ambroise Vollard and André Fontainas*, San Francisco.

1946   *To his wife and his friends*, Grasset, Paris, completed in 1949.

Some letters have been published in *Arts*, January 11, September 27, 1946, March 28, 1947. A complete edition is in preparation under the direction of J. Rewald and H. Rostrup.

OTHER MATERIAL OF GAUGUIN

ROBERT REY, *Onze menus de Paul G.*, Geneva, 1950.
RENÉ HUYGHE, *Le carnet de Paul G.*, Quatre Chemis, Paris, 1952.
BERNARD DORIVAL, *Carnet de Tahiti*, Quatre Chemins, Paris, 1954.

BIOGRAPHIES

The earliest were those by Charles Morice, in *Les Hommes d'Aujourd'hui,* published in 1891, 1920, and by Jean de Rotonchamp, published in Weimar, 1906, and in Paris, 1925, and by his daughter, Pola Gauguin, *Paul Gauguin Mon Père,* Edition de France Paris, 1938, transated from the Norwegian.
Others include those by:
ROBERT REY, Rieder, Paris, 1924, 1928, 1939.
CHARLES TERRASSE, Paris, 1927.
CHARLES KUNSTLER, *Gauguin: peintre maudit,* Floury, Paris, 1934, 1942, 1947.
HENRI PERRUCHOT, *Gauguin, sa vie ardente et misérable,* le Sillage, 1948.

MAURICE MALINGUE, *Gauguin le peintre et son oeuvre,* Presse de la Cité et Londres, Paris, 1948.
FRANK ELGAR, Paris, 1949.
CHARLES ESTIENNE, Skira, Geneva, 1953, all illustrations in color.
CHARLES CHASSÉ, *Gauguin et son temps,* Bibliothéque des Arts, Paris, 1955.
Volumes containing Gauguin plates include the following by:
PIERRE GIRIEUD, Album Druet, Paris, 1928.
LOUIS HAUTECOEUR, Skira, Geneva and Paris, 1942, all illustrations in color.
JOHN REWALD, Abrams, New York, 1954.

CATALOGUES

MARCEL GUÉRIN, *L'oeuvre gravé de Gauguin,* 2 volumes, Floury, Paris, 1927.

Since the exhibition of the works completed by Gauguin during his first trip to Tahiti, held at the salon of Durand-Ruel, November, 1893, and the sale of February 18, 1895, at the hotel Drouot, of works done by Gauguin before his first departure, the principal exhibitions have been:
Rétrospective du Salon d'Automne de 1906, catalogue with an introduction by CHARLES MORICE.
Sculptures de Gauguin, at the Luxembourg Museum, 1927, catalogue by MASSON and REY, followed by *Gauguin, sculpteur et graveur,* 1928, catalogue by MASSON and GUERIN.
Gauguin, ses amis, l'école de Pont-Aven et l'académie Julian, Galerie Beaux-Arts, February-March, 1934, catalogue by RAYMOND COGNIAT.

La vie ardente de Paul Gauguin, Galerie Wildenstein, Paris, 1936, catalogue by RAYMOND COGNIAT.
Exposition, Wildenstein Gallery, New York, March-April, 1936, April-May, 1946, catalogue by RAYMOND COGNIAT.
Exposition Ny Carlsberg Glyptotek, Copenhagen, May-June, 1948, including all items in Danish collections.
Exposition du Centenaire, Orangerie des Tuilieries, Paris, summer, 1949. Catalogue by J. LEYMARIE, introduction by R. HUYGHE. Repeated, Kunst Museum de Bâsel, November, 1949-January, 1950, with a complete catalogue.
Gauguin et le groupe de Pont-Aven, museum of Quimper, July-September, catalogue by G. MARTIN-MERY, introduction by R. HUYGHE.
Paul Gauguin, paintings, sculptures and engraving, Edinburgh festival, 1955, introduction and notes by DOUGLAS COOPER.

SPECIAL STUDIES

On Gauguin's techniques other than painting:
Ceramics: ROGER-MARX, *Revue encyclopédique,* September, 15, 1891.
Sculpture: LOUIS VAUXCELLES, *l'Art décoratif,* January, 1911; G. VARENNE, *la Renaissance,* December, 1927; ROBERT REY, *Art et Décoration,* February, 1928.
Graphic arts: DARAGNÈS, *Arts Graphiques,* n. 49, 1935; C. O. SCHNIEWIND, *Bulletin of the Art Institute of Chicago,* December, 1940

On the influence of Japanese painting on Gauguin's style:

C. MALTEE, *Emporium, January,* 1947.
On the various epochs of Gauguin's life:
Paul Gauguin à Copenhague, P. VASSEUR, *Revue de l'Art,* March, 1935. *Notes sur l'école dite de Pont-Aven,* EMILE BERNARD, *Mercure de France,* December, 1903. *Gauguin et le groupe de Pont-Aven,* CHARLES CHASSÉ, Floury,

Paris, 1921. « *Gauguin in Arles,* » Daniel C. Rich, *Bulletin,* of the Art Institute of Chicago, March, 1935. *Gauguin le solitaire du Pacifique* a pamphlet, Renée Hamon, Vigot, 1939. *Les démêlés de Gauguin avec les gendarmes et l'évêque des Isles Marquises,* Charles Chassé, Mercure de France, November 15, 1948.

On Gauguin's associates:

La moglie di Gauguin, G. Visenti, Florence, 1942. *Les amitiés du peintre Gauguin D.-de Monfried et ses reliques de Gauguin,* for the « Compagnons de St. Clément, » Paris, 1951. *Paul Gauguin. D. de Monfreid et leurs amis,* René Puig, la Tramontane, Perpignan, 1958. *Le peintre et collectionneur C.-L.E. Schuffenecker,* M. Boudot-Lamotte, *Amour de l'Art* 1935. *Gauguin et Mallarmé,* Charles Chassé, *Amour de l'Art,* 1922. *Gauguin et Victor Segalen,* Michel Florisoone, *Amour de l'Art,* December, 1938. « *Paul Gauguin and V. Segalen,* » A. Joly-Segalen, *Magazine of Art,* December, 1952. « *Camille Pissarro, His Work and Influence,* » John Rewald, *Burlington Magazine* June, 1938. *Van Gogh and Gauguin,* W. Hausenstein, Stuttgart-Berlin, 1914. *Gauguin i Van Gogh w. Arles,* K. Miterwa, Glos Plastikow, Poland, December, 1935. *Le carnet de Paul Gauguin,* René Huyghe, Quatre Chemins, Paris, 1952, on his relationship with Bernard, p. 36 *et seq.,* with Van Gogh, p. 50 *et seq.*

On Gauguin's style:

L'influence de Paul Gauguin, Maurice Denis, l'Occident, October, 1903 reprinted in *Théories,* Paris, 1912. *La Renaissance du sentiment classique,* Robert Rey, Beaux-Arts, 1931, the third chapter devoted to Gauguin. « *Sources of the Art of Gauguin from Java, Egypt and Ancient Greece,* » Bernard Dorival, *Burlington magazine,* April, 1951. *Die Entstehung des « Neuen Stils » in der fransosischen Malerei um* 1890, thesis, Friburg in Brisgau, November, 1954.

ILLUSTRATIONS

Adam and Eve	69
Alyscamps (The)	21
Around the Huts. Martinique	12
Barbaric Tales	83
« Be in love and you will be happy »	89
« Bonjour Monsieur Gauguin »	3
Breton Landscape	36
Breton Peasant Girls	10
Breton Village Covered by Snow	92
Calvary (The)	33
Christ on Mount Olive (Self-Portrait)	19
Family Schuffenecker (The)	38
Flowering of Spring	37
Garden in the Snow	9
Grasshoppers and the Ants (The)	13
Head of a Breton Girl	16
Heads of Breton Girls	25
Head of a Girl - Tahiti	43
Head of a Girl - Tahiti	61
Head of a Peasant Girl	27
Head of a Tahitian Woman	85
I Raro Te Oriri (Under the Pandanus)	51
Jacob Wrestling with the Angel	18
« La Belle Angèle »	22
« L'Arlésienne »	28
Manao Tupapau (The Spirit of the Dead)	56
Manao Tupapau (The Spirit of the Dead)	60
Man with a Cane	66
Man with an Axe	63
Market (The)	65
Martinique Women	11
Maternity	75
Menu Illustrated by Gauguin	71
Nafea Foa Ipoipo (When Will You Marry?)	54
Nave Nave Fenua (Delicious Earth)	58
Noa-Noa	59
On the Marquesas Islands	84
Oviri. Profile of Gauguin	88
Pape Moe (Holy Water)	47
Pastoral Scene, Martinique	14
Pissarro: Portrait of Gauguin; Gauguin: Portrait of Pissarro	8
Poèmes Barbares	82
Portrait of Madeleine Bernard	20
Portrait of Stéphane Mallarmé	40
Portrait of the Maternal Grandmother of Gauguin	6
Profile of the Artist	90
Profile of the Artist	91
Self-Portrait of Gauguin, before the Yellow Christ	32
Sewing	31
Siesta	64
Spirit of the Dead (The)	87
Spirit of the Dead Watching	45
Still Life with Oranges	34
Still Life with Head-Shaped Vase and Japanese Woodcut	35
Still Life with Sunflowers	80
Studies. Head of a Tahitian and a Profile Sketch	72
Study for Flowering of Spring	30
Study for the « Jeunes Garçons »	23
Study of a Nude	5
Swineherd with Yellow Pigs	17
Tahitian Girl	55
Tahitian Landscape	48
Tahitian Landscape with Girls	81
Tahitian Woman	42
Tahitian Women Bathing	50
Tahitian Women Bathing	76
Tahitian Women on the Beach	49
Tahitian Woman Sitting	68
Tahiti. Study	62
Te Aa No Areois (The Seed of the Areois)	53
Te Arii Vahine. (Woman of Royal Family)	67
Title of the Revue « Le Sourire »	57
Vahine Note vi (Girl with Mango)	52
Vairumati	77
Whence do we come? What Are we? Whither are we Going?	78-79
Woodcut of « Pape Moe »	46